The Complete Resume Guide: Landing That Coveted Job

ISBN: 979-8-9917974-8-1

Copyright 2025 by Susan Magras-Edwards

Written by Susan Magras-Edwards

Book design and layout by Susan M. Magras-Edwards/Magras Literary Entertainment (www.magrasliterary.com)

Published by Magras Literary Entertainment

Front and Back Cover Designs by Susan M. Magras-Edwards

Printed in the USA

Getting to Know the Author

Susan M. Edwards is a wife, mother, former educator, avid reader, writer, pet lover, and entrepreneur. She was born and raised on the island of St. Thomas, United States Virgin Islands. She now resides in sunny Southern California. She has two grown children, two daughters-in-law, two grandsons, and a vast extended family.

Susan spent many years working in the accounting field. Eventually, she became a teacher and worked for 17+ years. While she enjoyed teaching, she decided there were other ways she could teach and express her creativity and imagination without doing so in a classroom setting.

Through the years, Susan worked with many high school and college students, proofreading and editing their documents. She earned a bachelor's degree in business administration, a master's in organizational management (Human Resources), and a master's in education (Elementary Education).

Susan finally decided to publish her first book in 2019. Eventually, despite some setbacks, her book was first published in 2020, and printed copies became available in 2021. Her journey in writing continues with this and several other books, a cookbook, and multiple puzzle books.

The Complete Resume Guide: Landing That Coveted Job

What is a Resume?

A resume is typically a formal 1-2 page document when applying to jobs. A resume is an integral part of the search for a job. It is usually the first thing an employer sees. It is essential to make a great impression. This guide will take you through the critical steps you need to take and provide information you need to know. This list includes the best resume format, contact details, the headline you will use, and how to polish your resume to stand out to potential employers. This report will help you explore ways to avoid common mistakes and provide tips on making your resume stand out in online Application Tracking Systems (ATS).

Most job opportunities require applicants to submit their applications online. Since these submissions are made electronically, job seekers should be prepared to submit their applications, a high school or college transcript, and a resume.

Resumes are telling!

Hiring managers, recruits, or managers can look at your work history, job qualifications, skills, and education through your resume. In addition, your resume tells a story about your achievements, accomplishments, and awards. Combining these things can help you stand out from other applicants.

A Perfect Resume:

1. Demands the attention of readers
2. Highlights all the best that you offer
3. Demonstrate how and why you are the best fit for the job
4. It is free of spelling and grammatical errors and typos
5. Gets you the job interview for your dream job

The Best Resume Format (Which one?)

When you sit down to decide what you want to put in your resume, you'll want first to determine which resume format works best for you. There are three standard formats to choose from. They include chronological, functional, and combination formats.

Chronological

The chronological resume or reverse chronological format is the most common form many job seekers use. This format lists all your information in reverse chronological order. In other words, you start with the most recent place of employment and work your way backward to the oldest.

Functional

A functional resume format focuses on your skills. These are placed in a primary position at the top of the resume and highlight critical skills you possess versus listing the jobs held.

Combination

The combination format combines the two previous designs. First, you list your skills, and then you list your work history. The job you are seeking can help determine the format you use. Review the job requirements and decide on the most suitable design.

When preparing your resume, it is essential to ensure it is professional in appearance and content. It should also be relevant and tailored specifically to the job you are applying for. Hiring managers will often only look at the first page of a resume, so it needs to include all mandatory information at first glance, front and center.

Choose the Right Format For You

When determining the proper format for you, consider the following before making your decision:

Entry-Level: Functional

- Experienced: Chronological or combination
- Return to the Workforce: Functional or combination
- Career Change: Functional or combination

Contact Details:

Your contact information is the first thing a hiring manager will see at the top of your resume. You want this information to be accurate so the prospective employer can reach out to you should they wish to interview you for the position. This information is mandatory and should be professional, concise, straightforward, and up-to-date.

Your contact information should include the following:

- Your name, surname, address (City, State), phone number, and correct email address
- Your email address should sound and look professional. Create a new one, if necessary, one that will help you to stand out among other candidates. Depending on the hiring manager, an inappropriate email address could cost you the job.
- Many hiring managers may wish to do interviews online. These may take place through Skype, Zoom, or Teams. You can provide your LinkedIn or other social media links if you feel the relevant job information on those sites will help you stand out to potential employers. Please ensure your pages are as polished as your resume; in other words, clean them up before providing those links on your resume or application.
- Put all your information in one or two lines to save space; be concise.

Resume Headline:

The resume headline comes immediately after your contact information. This section is your first chance to make a good impression on hiring managers. A short, compelling resume highlights your professional background. It combines keywords that bring attention to essential information for the reader that will immediately be associated with you as they review your resume. Your resume headline should be short but pack a punch so you will grab the hiring manager's attention.

Write an effective headliner that hooks readers, keeping them engaged by doing the following:

- Review job postings and compare them with your skills and experience. Make a list of the overlapping areas.
- Focus on two or three items that reflect your most substantial assets. These should be assets directly related to the job you are applying for. You should have multiple versions of your resume available if you qualify for various positions. Just remember which one you sent to each prospective employer. I recommend printing a copy of each application and attaching a plain copy of your resume. Doing this will help you to remember which one to bring to an interview. Note:

Always print your resume on good-quality business paper.

- Combine your key selling points in a concise, compelling tagline that grabs readers' attention.

Resume Summary:

After creating your resume headline, focus on building your brand. Your resume and social media platforms should reflect your brand. A Resume Summary is a brief description of your career. It falls under your contact information and your resume headline. Your summary should tell who you are and what you bring to the table in an engaging, effective, and concise way.

The summary should include the following:

- Your relevant areas of expertise
- The job-related and transferable skills that you bring to the job
- What you have achieved in your previous job

The resume summary explains why or how you would be an excellent fit for the job. Remember that recruiters and hiring managers often only spend a short time on your resume. You want your resume summary to buzz with effectiveness so you can experience success in your job search. You want them to spend as much time as possible on your resume so they can see whether you are indeed a perfect fit for the organization.

Work Experience:

One critical thing recruiters and hiring managers do is review a resume, looking for relatable skills and experiences to help them determine whether a candidate is qualified or would be the right fit. Some candidates need to realize just how important it is to have the most critical work experience visible to recruiters.

The work experience section should include the following:
- Current and previous job titles
- Current and prior companies/organizations
- Dates of employment
- Brief descriptions of each job

List your current or previous professional experience first. Then, list your previous experience following a reverse-chronological order (If this is your preferred format). Focus on achievements rather than daily tasks and duties. Keep this section concise, informative, and engaging. Cut out empty phrases that take space and start each bullet point with an action. Use effective action verbs when completing the bulleted job section under work experience. Using compelling action verbs will gain the attention of hiring managers—action verbs up your game by calling attention to what you have done. Action Verbs will inject life into essential aspects of your previous job experiences.

The following are some action verbs you can use:
- Introduced
- Authored
- Reconciled
- Resolved
- Analyzed
- Consolidated
- Launched

Research specific action verbs that apply to your experiences and job search online.

Soft Skills Verses Hard Skills

Soft Skills:

Soft skills are those that show your personality traits and attributes. Such skills include leadership, creativity, communication, time management, organizational skills, and teamwork.

Hard Skills:

Hard skills are those learned on the job or through educational training. These demonstrate the qualifications and skills you possess to help you carry out daily tasks to excel in your role. Such skills include data analysis and marketing.

Transferable Skills:

Transferable skills are used in multiple job roles and career fields. These skills can be hard or soft but can play an important role when changing careers or applying for a job that does not explicitly match your past experiences. Such skills include critical thinking and computer skills, technical backgrounds, and problem-solving.

Formatting Your Skills

To make this resume section easier, create a list of all your skills. List your top three or four. The key is convincing hiring managers that you deserve an opportunity to interview. Your skills should be listed in bulleted format.

Education:

Putting your education on your resume ranks right up

top with your work experience. Education is the second most crucial part of your professional experience and should fall right behind the work experience section. Note: This will likely be first on your resume if this is the first job you are applying for.

It is essential to provide employers with crucial information regarding your educational experience.

1. The name of the school - Most recent first
2. The school's location
3. Your degrees, diplomas, and any certification obtained (Start with the highest degree you have earned)
4. Your major(s) and minor(s)
5. Graduation completion date(s) - High school students should include their expected graduation date
6. Once you have completed college, only include your high school information if specifically asked.
7. Academic Honors - include Cum Laude, Summa Cum Laude, Magna Cum Laude, and Dean's List information.
8. Licenses and Certifications
   a. Name of license/certification
   b. Institution of certification
   c. Location

d. Certification date or "in progress" if not completed
9. Training
10. Online courses
11. Seminars
12. Continuing Education
13. Work Shops
14. Presentations

Membership and Organizational Affiliations

Membership in a group or organization, mainly if relevant to your career path, can set you apart from other candidates seeking the same job opportunity. You should include the organization's name, title, and specific contributions.

Note: Use this section to note your GPA, any relevant coursework, honors and awards, extracurricular activities, and other information related to the job you are seeking.

The Importance of Having Multiple Resume Versions

Fine-tuning your resume to fit each job opportunity you apply to is so important! You want your resume to match specific words in the job description to increase your chances of receiving an invitation to interview.

Technology and Its Impact on the Job Market

In recent years, Artificial Intelligence, or AI, has been on the rise and is used in multiple ways by various industries. This is why It is no surprise that employers are using ATS to assist them in the hiring process. In 1748, Benjamin Franklin said in his work, "Advice to Young Tradesman," that "time is money." Hiring managers and recruiters are finding ways to reduce their workloads. Doing this includes using artificial intelligence and other technological means to help them focus on finding the ideal candidate. Employers often use AI to conduct various behavioral assessments to determine whether a candidate fits the job and the organization.

Polished Resume Design:

Ensuring your resume contains all pertinent information necessary to help you secure your new position is essential. However, creating an appealing resume may increase your chances of getting it read. Attracting prospective employers' attention at first glance can make the difference in you landing that coveted interview.

Layout:

Choosing your resume's layout will determine its content's structure and organization. There are two layout forms to choose from when setting up your resume: one- or two-column.

The one-column resume is a standard in the industry and lists all information in a page-wide or full-width column. This layout emphasizes content and is the most compatible with ATS software.

The two-column resume separates information into two smaller columns on each page. This format allows for more flexibility with the document structure. The candidate can organize their data more modern and visually attractive.

You must determine which design layout suits you and the jobs you are applying for.

Fonts:

When determining which font to use, remember that this can significantly impact your resume's overall impression to hiring managers. Consider opting for a safe, simple, professional look using fonts that will likely stand out in the ATS software.

Examples include using Sans Serif Fonts such as the following:

- Calibri
- Arial
- Helvetica

These examples will help your resume look finished, polished, and professional.

Colors:

The color(s) you use in your resume can significantly impact its success and your securing that coveted interview. Colors in a resume should have the desired effect you wish them to have. The colors you choose should fit the target industry you are applying to.

For example, for jobs in finance, banking, or law, you should consider using conservative colors such as black, gray, or blue. Consider using more fun color choices for employment in marketing, social media, creative design, or an artistic field. Blue, gray, green, and purple may suit these careers.

Note: Avoid bright or vibrant colors such as red, pink, yellow, or neon.

White Spaces:

There should be some white spaces in your resume so they can help improve readability. Your goal is to assist readers in navigating the content in the resume.

To optimize white spaces in your resume, consider the following:

- Adjust the line spacing to at least one inch between lines
- Increase spacing after each paragraph. Do this consistently throughout the resume
- Use easy-to-read font sizes such as 10 or 12
- Set margins between 0.5 to one inch

Optimizing Your Resume for ATS

ATS stands for Applicant Tracking System. Employers use this system to receive, organize, and sort job applications, scoring them based on keywords and other essential factors. I have applied for jobs in the past where hundreds of other applicants were vying for the same position. It is understandable why employers would use ATS. Hiring managers or recruiters would require more time to read hundreds of applications and resumes. Employers can whittle down the number of applicants with ATS by selecting the most qualified. Thus, it is essential to format your resume so the ATS does not weed out your application before it even gets in front of hiring managers.

The ATS searches for keywords that match job descriptions. Some of these keywords are as follows:

- Accounting
- Acquisition
- Business Development
- Business Management
- Coding
- Computer Design
- Computer Science

- Content Management
- Office Manager
- Financial Management
- Graphic Designer
- Marketing

These are just a few. Review the job announcement to ensure your resume identifies explicitly your skills and experiences that match the job description.

Here are some tips you can follow to ensure your resume is formatted correctly:

- Avoid using graphics, including text boxes, tables, photographs, and icons. Be aware that ATS cannot read these, so some of your information may get skipped during the screening process.
- Proofread your resume multiple times. Have a professional proofreader, if necessary, review your document to ensure it is error-free. The ATS software cannot recognize typos or spelling errors on your resume. It will make content comparisons, looking for matching keywords that fit the job description.
- Use a clean resume design; a minimalist resume usually works best with most ATS software. Keeping

things clean will likely improve your chances of surpassing the screening filters.

Avoiding Common yet Avoidable Mistakes on Your Resume

When you put your resume together, you must ensure it is spotless. One simple error can have a significant impact on your chances. Your goal is to show your best professional traits without giving the impression that you don't care or are unqualified for a position because your resume needs to be formatted or written better.

Simple mistakes such as spelling, wrong email addresses, incomplete or vague summaries, or not being specific enough can kill your job search before it even has a chance.

Resume Builders and Examples

Why reinvent the wheel? You can access multiple resume examples and programs on the World Wide Web. Any one of these programs can help you create a winning resume. Referencing pre-written examples you find online can save you time and move you closer to securing your coveted job.

You will still be responsible for the content and format of your resume.

What Is A Resume Builder?

A resume builder is an online tool that helps job seekers quickly create and prepare a professional resume for free. There are many options to choose from. Some are free, while others require you to pay a fee. Which one, if any, you decide to utilize will depend on how much help you need. Anyone can benefit from using a resume builder app. Since you are applying for a job, you will want it to be professional-looking to show hiring managers that you are serious about wanting the job and willing to go the extra mile by providing a well-planned resume.

How Does A Resume Builder Work?

In a resume builder app, they give you the option of selecting a resume template. The software will build you a professional-looking resume in just a few minutes by answering critical questions about your work experience, education, and skills; the software will create a professional-looking resume in just a few minutes. Be sure to proofread your resume and review the information you entered for accuracy. Always check for errors. Include relevant links, important dates, and other pertinent information. Double-check the spacing for consistency.

File Formats for Your Resume

Regardless of how you create your resume, whether on a resume builder or your own, review the submission requirements the prospective employer has indicated in the job announcements. Many will ask you to submit your resume in PDF or Word format. You will want to follow the employer's instructions. When there are no instructions from the employer, use the PDF format, as it is the universally accepted way to submit your resume. This is because PDFs are easier to read than other formats, and the 'look' of your resume will be preserved. Sometimes, when I send Word documents, the formatting will be off depending on which version of Word is being used. Also, for me, it is a way to preserve the integrity of my document.

CVs: What Are They?

A Curriculum Vitae (CV) is a short, written summary of a person's career, qualifications, and education. It is a more detailed account of your work/career history than you would find in a resume. Some employers may request a CV versus a resume, so read the job announcement thoroughly. The CV presents a complete history of your academic credentials, so the length of the document is variable. In contrast, a resume offers a concise picture of your skills and qualifications for a specific position, so size tends to be shorter and dictated by years of experience, so they are around 1-2 pages.

Individuals seeking fellowships, grants, postdoctoral positions, teaching/research positions in postsecondary institutions, or high-level research positions in the industry use CVs. Graduate school applications typically request a CV, but they generally seek a resume that includes any publications and descriptions of research projects.
SVs generally:

- Emphasizes academic accomplishments
- used when applying for positions in academia, fellowships, and grants

- The length depends upon experience and includes a complete list of publications, posters, and presentations
- It always begins with education and can include the name of the advisor and dissertation title or summary.
- Also used for merit/tenure review and sabbatical leave.

As a former educator, I know that a CV is beneficial when applying for a position in education, particularly in upper management. Other roles may include, but are not limited to, researcher, healthcare provider, and professor. The CV format is like a resume, but there are some differences you should be aware of.

Headings may include the following:

- Contact information
- Education
- Academic and related employment
- Presentations
- Grants
- Fellowships
- Awards
- Certifications
- Licenses
- Skills
- References

Cover Letters

Many businesses will request that applicants submit a cover letter with their application and resume. A cover letter is a business letter that summarizes your relevant work experience and skills, at the same time providing a glimpse into your personality and writing ability. The cover letter is the place to share why you would be an excellent fit for the position you are applying for.

A cover letter is essential to your application, and you should consider what you want to say. Similarly to making a good impression with your resume, you will enjoy your cover letter to stand out. Your impressive cover letter can motivate and convince a hiring manager to read your resume.

A cover letter should include the following:

- Header
- Introductory statement
- Explanation as to why you are the right candidate
- Call to action

The ideal length of a cover letter should be limited to one page. Consider how many cover letters and resumes a hiring manager must review. Be as brief as you reasonably can, but use powerful wording. The ideal cover letter will be no longer than ¾ of a page and be between 250 - 500 words. It should also be appropriately formatted. You want to present your most professional-looking letter, including using the right fonts (See above for tips about fonts you can use). I use 1" borders on all sides of my cover letters. As always, proofread your work before sending it. Always check for typos, spelling, and grammatical errors. Check whether the employer has requested you submit your cover letter in a particular format. If no information about the employer's preference is available, submit it in PDF format; if you are unsure how to write your cover letter or need some guidance, research online, as there are plenty of examples.

Portfolios

Some jobs may require you to have a portfolio. A portfolio may include the following:

- Career summary
- Philosophy Statement
- A short biography
- Resume
- Marketable skills and abilities

- Professional accomplishments
- Samples of your work
- Awards and honors
- Transcripts, degrees, licenses, and certifications
- Professional development
- Volunteer/community service
- References/testimonials

What Type of Employee?

When applying for a job, you should know whether you want part-time or full-time employment. What type of employee are you looking to be? Full-time employees typically work 30 to 40 hours per week and receive benefits and employee incentives. A full-time employee can also be salaried but work more than the typical 40-hour maximum week. Part-time employees work at most 30 hours per week and typically will not receive any medical, dental, vision, or other benefits offered to full-time employees.

Some places hire freelancers, consultants, seasonal employees, or independent contractors. Many of these individuals are not employees of the organization and will often receive a 1099 form for reporting their earnings. Companies will hire these individuals to save on payroll expenses but also because they need someone with specialized services for a shorter period. You must decide if you want to go this route when job hunting.

What Are Your Goals and Aspirations?

Evaluating your goals and career aspirations will help guide you in the right direction when job hunting. Only you can decide the path you wish to take and what it will take to accomplish your desired goals. If you are looking to enter a particular industry and need more experience, consider shadowing an employee who does what you want to do. You must also assess your current experience and education levels and determine whether you will need additional training or education. I have always found that networking with friends, family, and coworkers is invaluable. Attending business mixers is also a great way to meet people in different industries and ask questions about the pros and cons of working in that industry and what it takes to do what they do.

Determining the Right Time to Make Your Move

Whenever I have changed jobs or made career moves, I have taken time to evaluate my current position first. I try not to allow my emotions to get in the way of making sound decisions, although we often make career changes because we are unhappy, feel stagnant, or are likely that the job may no longer be the right fit for the direction we want to go. Before deciding, ask yourself the following questions:

- Am I giving my best daily?
- Is my job making me sick or stressed?
- Am I satisfied with my salary/pay rate?
- Is this my dream job?
- Do I have a good work/life balance?
- Am I feeling accomplished?

These are just a few questions you can ask yourself. Thoroughly examine each question and be honest with yourself about your responses.

Where To Look For Jobs

Job seekers are always looking for opportunities. When I started my career, newspapers advertised jobs under the classified pages. As technology changed and developed, so did how people looked for employment. Today, the easiest and most effective way to search for job openings is by conducting online searches. Job seekers can post their resumes and search for jobs on many websites. Job seekers can also go directly to the websites of many employers and search for jobs there. Create a profile, username, and password, and enter your information into the system. Once you finish, you can find job opportunities right at your fingertips.

Interviews

Before a job interview, you should prepare by researching the company, reading the job description, preparing the answers to common interview questions, and creating queries to ask the prospective employer. Remember that not only are they interviewing you, but you are interviewing them.

Find someone to practice the interview with. If no one is available to assist you, practice on your own. Interviewers commonly use the STAR method to ask behavioral questions.

The STAR method is an interview technique that provides a straightforward format for telling a story by laying out the Situation, Task, Action, and Result.

- Situation: Set the scene and give the necessary details of your example.
- Task: Describe what your responsibility was in that situation.
- Action: Explain exactly what steps you took to address it.
- Result: Share what outcomes your actions achieved.

Some samples of those types of questions are as follows:

- Tell me about a time when you
- Describe a work situation where you
- Give me an example of when you
- Have you ever
- What do you do when

Writing Your Questions for The Job Interview

As I mentioned, you should arrive at an interview with questions to ask the interviewer. Some common questions are as follows:

1. What are you looking for in an ideal candidate?
2. Can you describe a typical day in this role?

3. What is the working culture of the organization?
4. What are some challenges of this job?
5. What is your favorite thing about working for this company?

Be On Time!

One of job seekers' most significant mistakes is showing up to an interview late. Plan your route, leave early, confirm the interview time and location, and know who you are meeting with if that information is available. The onus is on you to ensure you are prepared in every way. You want to appear organized, professional, and excited about the opportunity.

Tips for In-Person Interviews

Take some time to prepare for your interview. You will want to appear relaxed and ready to speak about yourself and answer questions. Remember, this should be an exciting time! You will want to dress professionally by appearing in a business outfit. Press your clothes so you don't appear wrinkled. Choose neutral colors and avoid using overpowering cologne or perfumes. You want to present your best professional image and leave a positive and lasting impression on the interviewer(s). Practice your body language and vocal delivery. Speak slowly, loudly, and clearly. Try to limit or eliminate the "ums," "ahs," and "likes" that we will often say when thinking of what we want to say. Pause, reflect, and continue. Be sure to sit up straight. I have practiced in front of a mirror before and found it helpful.

Going on a job interview can be intimidating, so once you are done, focus on the questions one at a time. Pause before answering, allow yourself to laugh, and let the interviewer lead you through the interview.

Remote Interviews

Since the pandemic, many employers have shifted to interviewing candidates online using Zoom, Teams, or other video methods. Remember that even though the interview is remote, you still need to act and dress the part of a professional. If the interview is by phone, ensure your cell phone is charged. If you use your computer, test your internet connection, camera, and audio. Prepare early so you don't feel embarrassed because your technology is malfunctioning. Set up a clean and clear area for your interview. Be sure it is a quiet space where you will not be interrupted by pets, children or other adults. Ensure that the background looks professional.

After The Interview, What's Next?

After the interview, ask the interviewer for their contact information and the next steps in the hiring process if they still need to discuss this with you. Send a thank-you message within 24 hours of your interview. Your message should emphasize your continued interest in the job and the company. Doing this will help keep you front and center in employers' minds, and they move forward with interviewing other candidates. Sending a digital message also opens up the door for additional communication between the interviewer and yourself.

Conclusion

Having a premiere resume occurs because of the time, effort, and commitment you put into it. Once you have written your professional resume, it can change the trajectory of your job search and, eventually, your career when you land that coveted job you have dreamed of.

I remember my first resume as if it were yesterday. If this is your first resume, contact a professional to help you prepare a resume that will bring you closer to achieving your goal of finding the right job that suits you. Your resume should make you shine and stand out among other candidates during your job search.

References

Franklin, Benjamin. 1748. "Advice to Young Tradesman"

https://www.indeed.com/career-advice/resumes-cover-letters/10-resume-writing-tips

Resume Tips to Land a Job in 2025 (From a Hiring Manager)

www.merriam-webster.com

OTHER BOOKS BY THIS AUTHOR

STORIES

- CUPCAKE ISLAND: THE KIDNAPPED PRINCE (2024 REVISION COMING SOON)
- THE HIBISCUS CLUB MYSTERIES: THE MISSING NOTEBOOK (COMING SOON IN 2025)
- MAKING FAST FOOD: A CARIBBEAN-BASED CHILDREN'S STORY (COMING SOON IN 2025)
- ENCHANTED SNAKE ISLAND: THE MISSING TIARA (COMING SOON IN 2025)
- JOURNEY FROM DEPRESSION TO FREEDOM

COOKBOOKS

- CARIBBEAN MEDLEY: A COMPILATION OF CARIBBEAN-AMERICAN RECIPES
- DESSERTS AND BREAD (COMING SOON IN 2025)

INFORMATIONAL BOOKS

- CREATIVE WRITING COURSE
- CREATIVE WRITING COURSE WORKBOOK

PUZZLE BOOKS:

- KID'S CHRISTMAS ACTIVITY BOOK
- KID'S THANKSGIVING PUZZLE BOOK
- KID'S HALLOWEEN PUZZLE BOOK
- CHRISTMAS WORD SEARCH
- BIBLE-THEMED WORD SEARCH

- HALLOWEEN PUZZLE BOOK
- THANKSGIVING PUZZLE BOOK
- VALENTINE'S PUZZLE BOOK
- MUSIC AND INSTRUMENTS PUZZLE BOOK
- FOODS, FOODS, FOODS PUZZLE BOOK
- DOGS AND CATS PUZZLE BOOK
- FOURTH OF JULY AND SUMMER PUZZLE BOOK
- SEASONS PUZZLE BOOK
- SPORTS PUZZLE BOOK

FOLLOW US ON:

- **FACEBOOK:**
  - MAGRAS LITERARY ENTERTAINMENT
  - THE HIBISCUS CLUB MYSTERIES
  - THE TRAVELER'S DETECTIVE AGENCY BOOKS
- **INSTAGRAM:**
  - MAGRASLITERARY
  - HIBISCUSCLUBMYSTERIES
  - TRAVELERSDETECTIVEAGENCYBOOKS
- **Amazon:**
  - Susan M. Magras-Edwards

WRITING SERVICES:

Visit us at www.magrasliterary.com for your writing needs. You can also email us at magrasliterary@gmail.com or connect with us via our website. Please email us to receive our monthly newsletter filled with updates.

www.ingramcontent.com/pod-product-compliance
Lightning Source LLC
Chambersburg PA
CBHW071448040426
42445CB00012BA/1481